IN THE NAME OF HONOR

戦い

IN THE FACE OF BATTLE

男の心

IN THE HEART OF ONE MAN

侍魂

LIVES THE SOUL OF A WARRIOR

THE
LAST
SAMURAI

武士道

SCREENPLAY WRITTEN BY JOHN LOGAN AND
MARSHALL HERSKOVITZ & EDWARD ZWICK
FOREWORD BY EDWARD ZWICK
PHOTOGRAPHS BY DAVID JAMES

I'VE ALWAYS LOVED STORIES ABOUT THE END OF THINGS. Perhaps because they confirm some inner understanding we all have that nothing lasts forever. It's as if there is something comforting, restful even, in an ineluctable march toward a fated end.

Interestingly enough, this has been a classic theme not only of the Western, but also of the samurai movie. As often as not, these films have portrayed heroes who stand tall against the tide of time, men of action whose values are no longer held in the same esteem as in the past, yet who are willing to lay their lives on the line for those values, even against impossible odds. In fact, they have no choice; for them, life has no meaning unless lived according to a code. Whether called honor, dignity, authenticity, or *Bushido*, it leads them, sooner or later, into a confrontation with the decidedly less philosophical, utterly pragmatic demands of the world. And almost always to a tragic end.

FOREWORD

The end of the nineteenth century was a time of wrenching transition for so many societies, but none more so than for the Japanese. For hundreds of years theirs had been a closed, almost hermetic society, deliberately cut off from the outside world. But everything changed the moment Commodore Perry sailed into Yokohama harbor with his gunboats and demanded Japan open to trade with the United States—or he would burn its cities to the ground. Japan would join the world beyond its borders, or it would perish.

Overnight, the rickshaw and the oxcart made way for the steam locomotive. The government collapsed, styles and manners changed beyond recognition, and a modern, conscript army was deemed necessary to defend the newly restored emperor from the mechanized forces of the Western powers. The implications of such sweeping change were particularly wrenching for the samurai, whose sacred duty had always been to defend the emperor. Once the most revered (and feared) class, they now found themselves with no real position in the new order.

Many samurai joined the new government; some accepted money in exchange for control of their lands. But others would not, or could not. To them, the obvious rewards of the new and modern could not outweigh the more subtle loss of the ancient and the traditional.

And so they rebelled.

America, meanwhile, had endured its own rebellion. The Civil War, fought to save a nation, had also shattered a generation. Those veterans not wounded outright would forever bear the scars of five horrible years of fighting. For many of these warriors, the transition to civilian life was impossible. And so they returned to the army and went West, lured by the promise of open land and simple truths. But too soon, they found themselves embroiled in another war, this time with the Indian Nations. It, too, was a war won at a terrible cost.

Which brings us to *The Last Samurai,* in which we imagine that one of these warriors kept moving on—hoping that time and distance might obliterate the memory of all he had seen and done—until he found that, in continuing West, he had wound up East. In Japan. And there, in the least likely place imaginable, he encounters another such warrior, buffeted by history and progress. In the middle of another civil war, these two men meet first as enemies, only to end up fighting, side by side, in defense of an ineffable common ground—the only thing they still consider worth fighting for: their honor.

Was there ever a man named Nathan Algren? No. But were there American military men in Japan at this time? Yes, and French, and German, too. Did an important samurai leader rebel? His name was Saigo Takamori, and a large statue in downtown Tokyo attests to his importance in Japanese history. But the notion that the two came together in common cause is a literary fancy.

Why then partake of so much fact for the sake of a fiction? Why worry about anachronisms, or devote so much attention to period detail? Because to place a story in an accurately rendered context at once plants its feet on the firm ground of history, and at the same time endows it with the epic feel that only such history can provide. In this regard, we are brazenly emulating the greatest writers of all time—Dumas, Shakespeare, Tolstoy—shameless pilferers of history, all.

Twice before I have filmed stories set in this historical moment. Each has naturally presented its own set of challenges, but one task unites them all: to tell a story that is at once recognizable to a contemporary audience and at the same time true to the spirit of an age. This is a daunting notion—that a film be made to feel immediate while taking place in a period its makers have never known. My only hope when faced with such an undertaking is to pray for a kind of alchemy—of research, of language, and of imagination.

And also for a lot of help.

Fortunately I found it in a team of uniquely gifted filmmakers, who also turned out to be as dogged and unafraid as they were talented. Each of them believed, as I do, that a story is inseparable from its production: that its strength derives from the authenticity of its sets and costumes as much as from its acting and staging, and that the quality of light on a face can provide a poetry that far exceeds any words spoken. In fact, the months spent gathering original source material, the care given to the construction of its surfaces, the selection of its fabrics, props, and weapons all provide a bedrock on which the actors stand. The emotional truth felt by an audience is really a reaction to the combustion of all these elements coming together at once, and then captured at twenty-four frames per second.

I literally cannot imagine this film without John Toll's cinematography, Lilly Kilvert's design, or Ngila Dickson's wardrobe. David Gulick's props were more than appropriate; they were inspired. Paul Lombardi's effects and Nick Powell's stunts were somehow at once terrifying *and* safe. Lois Burwell turned back time on each face she touched. And none of it would have happened without Chuck Mulvehill's guidance, Paula Wagner's unshakable confidence, Nilo Otero's stewardship, and Kevin de la Noy's compassionate tyranny. Ken Watanabe and Hiroyuki Sanada suffered my cross-cultural lapses with generosity and good humor, and at the same time took on the mantel of technical advisors by virtue of their considerable expertise in all things samurai. And always there was Yoko Narahashi, whose belief in the commonality of all men and all nations served as an inspiration for us all. Oh, yes, and did I mention a crew of two thousand, from thirty countries, spread out over three continents…

And yet this film was imagined long before any of these talented people signed on. By John Logan. By Marshall Herskovitz. And by Tom Cruise. And then put together with consummate artistry by Steven Rosenblum.

The making of a film has, perhaps a bit romantically, been described as the voyage of a ship. If there be any truth in this metaphor, then many times in its making I have imagined myself standing at its prow, utterly lost, without compass or plan, more than a little mad, howling profanities into the wind. Yet, each time I threatened to wreck us all on the shoals of disaster, one of these extra-ordinary comrades was there to right my course.

Edward Zwick
Santa Monica, California, 2003

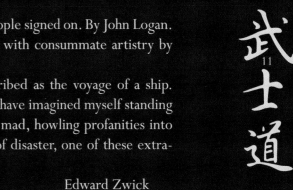

11

MORE THAN A YEAR AGO, it was suggested that a book be created to include select images from the *The Last Samurai*, to provide a bit of historical context for the film, and perhaps even to document a few of the particular challenges of its production. No one could have known, at the time, just how overwhelming those challenges would be, nor how much work it might take to assemble such a volume. Certainly no one could have envisioned just how many striking images David James would capture during the course of principal photography.

ACKNOWLEDGMENTS

Slowly, though, the book began to take on a life of its own—as a few determined people set out to record the artistry of seven or eight hundred more. No single page of this book could possibly have happened without the combined efforts of each and every member of the production: it's one thing to marvel at a silhouetted image of a horse and rider, but quite another to understand the kind of infrastructure working tirelessly (and anonymously) just outside the periphery of the frame. Consider the silhouetted rider in question. Long before this famous Japanese actor could appear on the set, he required a visa, then a plane ticket, then food, housing, and transportation. He trained with an English horse master, had his special make-up done by an Irish artist, and wore a costume designed and built in New Zealand. He holds a prop sword manufactured in Australia. He is riding a horse that was trained for months by Spanish horsemen so as not to fear gunfire and explosions. And he would not be in silhouette at all, but for an artful layer of smoke created by an American special effects team, then backlit by the grips and electricians. In fact, the forest in which the rider stands was designed and built by the construction crew. The same collaboration holds true for every frame...

And so, to each of the remarkable people—far too numerous to list here—whose brilliance and professionalism informs these images, we say thank you, and hope the finished film can somehow begin to justify the intensity of their labors. As for those whose efforts yielded this volume, we mention them here in very special gratitude:

Graham Larson, Lee Anne De Vette, Michael Doven, Skye Van Raalte-Herzog, Melanie O'Brien, Terry J. Erdmann, Diane Nelson, Debbie Miller, Maggie Schmidt, Jess Garcia, John Eakin, Massey Rafani, Greg Moore, Steve Fogelson, Noriko Okuda, Ai Hashimoto, Jack Teed, Vivek Mathur, James Verdesoto, Rachel Aberly, Grady Lee, Sophia Cook, Cedar McClure, Josh Gummersall, Troy Putney, Geoff Pattison, and Josh Breslow.

武士道

12

ONLY OUT OF HONOR
DO YOU EARN THE RIGHT
TO BE KNOWN AS SAMURAI.
THE WAY OF THE SAMURAI

FADE IN:

A WHITE TIGER

Surrounded by dark shapes with spears.
The TIGER's eyes burn as he lunges at
one tormentor, claws at another. Suddenly,
the TIGER leaps over them all and BURSTS
INTO FLAME.

THE FACE OF A JAPANESE MAN

Sits up INTO FRAME. He is KATSUMOTO…
We will come to know him later.

武
士
道

17

INT. CONVENTION HALL (SAN FRANCISCO) - DAY

WINCHESTER REP
One of the most decorated warriors
this country has ever known. Winner of
the Medal of Honor for his gallantry on
the hallowed ground of Gettysburg…

He is late of the 7th Cavalry and their
triumphant campaign against the most
savage of the Indian Nations. Ladies and
gentlemen, I present to you: Captain
Nathan Algren!

武士道

EXT. SHIP (OCEAN) - DAY

A steamship churns its way across the great Pacific.

ALGREN (V.O.)
July 12, 1876. There is some comfort in
the emptiness of the sea. No past, no
future. Just a vast oblivion. I have been
hired to help suppress the rebellion of
yet another leader. Apparently this is
the only job for which I am suited. I am
beset by the ironies of my life.

INT./EXT. RICKSHAW/TOKYO STREETS - DAY

GRAHAM

Twenty years ago, this was a sleepy little
town. Now look at it. It's like the modern
and the ancient competing for the soul of
Japan. It's quite marvelous actually.
                    (sees two Japanese men
                    in Western clothing)
Oh, look at that, that's good there. That's
why the samurai are so upset. It was their job
to keep everyone out, and now Omura has
welcomed in a world of foreigners. Lawyers
from France, engineers from Germany,
architects from Holland…and now of
course warriors from America. I came over
with the British trade mission, oh…years
ago. I was soon relieved of my position.
                    (off Algren's look)
I had an unfortunate tendency to tell the
truth in a country where no one ever says
what they mean. So now I very accurately
translate other people's lies.

THE ISOLATION OF JAPAN

In 1543, a Chinese ship arrived in Japanese waters. On board were three Portuguese adventurers, believed to be the first Europeans to visit Japan. At the time, their visit seemed to have little significance; they sold two guns to a government official and went home. But when that minor sale became public knowledge in the West, it opened the door to a lucrative market for international trade. Western merchants quickly set sail for the island nation, closely followed by Christian missionaries. And for the next ninety-three years, business thrived between Japan and the West.

The government of the ruling *shogun,* or "supreme military commander," initially welcomed the Westerners, but ultimately came to worry about their influence on Japanese society. The shogunate maintained strict political and social controls over Japan's tiered class system. Strict rules prevented rising above one's class and marrying between classes. Those rules kept the populace in place, but could not contain widespread poverty, or the discontent that accompanied it.

From the time of their arrival in the sixteenth century, the Westerners had been influencing Japanese thought. In particular, the missionaries were successful in converting many in the lower classes to Christianity, causing the *shogun* to fear that his absolute control would be undermined. He attempted to counteract their influence with an edict banning the religion. It had little effect. Then, in 1637, insurrection among some peasant converts to Christianity forced the *shogun* to take harsher measures. After expelling or killing all of the missionaries and foreign merchants, the *shogun* closed Japan's shores to the rest of the world. Henceforth, only two ships per year—one from longtime trading partner China, and one from the Netherlands (whose representatives had persuaded the Japanese government that they were the leading power in the West)—would be allowed to approach.

The island nation remained in this state of isolation—known as *sakoku* (literally, "closed country")—for the next 250 years.

22

武士道

EXT. IMPERIAL PALACE - DAY

Algren, Graham and Bagley approach the ancestral palace.

GRAHAM
For two thousand years no emperor
was even seen by a commoner. You have
to realize what an absolute treat
this is, what an honor. It's all highly
ritualized of course. You may look at
him, but do not speak, unless spoken
to, obviously. If he stands you must
bow, if he bows you must bow lower.
Do I look presentable? Haven't worn
this in a decade. Rather snug around
the midriff.

EXT. PARADE GROUND - DAY

ALGREN
What can the general tell me about
this man, this samurai, Katsumoto?

ALGREN (V.O.)
He seems to have great knowledge
of Katsumoto and his rebellion. We
will count on his help when facing
the samurai.

ALGREN
Who supplies their weapons?

GRAHAM
Katsumoto no longer dishonors
himself by using firearms, you see.

ALGREN
He uses no firearms?

GRAHAM
(adding a flourish)
You see, to those who honor the
old ways, Katsumoto is a hero.

Algren looks at Hasegawa, who nods back politely.

ALGREN
How well does he know this man?

GRAHAM
Well, the general and Katsumoto
fought together for the emperor.

ALGREN
He fought with the samurai?

Graham looks at Algren.

GRAHAM
He is samurai.

THE OPENING OF JAPAN

The rise of international trade may seem a curious backdrop for an action film, but nineteenth-century Japan's growing engagement with the world economy was a subject that excited the filmmakers.

"The importance of Japan to the Western powers cannot be overstated, because Japan was a way station to China," John Logan says. "Everyone wanted the China trade because it was so valuable. China was Eldorado. Japan offered a way station with coal. Once America had steamships, they needed coal to go from San Francisco to Hawaii, then from Hawaii to Japan, and then on to China."

The need for a coaling station was not lost on the fifteenth president of the United States, Millard Fillmore. In his message to Congress on April 5, 1852, the president stated that it would be in America's best interests to open a "mutually beneficial intercourse" with the island nation. Fillmore continued, "I have ordered an appropriate naval force to Japan, under the command of a discreet and intelligent officer, to obtain from that government some relaxation of the inhospitable and anti-social system which it has pursued for two centuries."

Commodore Matthew C. Perry was that "discreet and intelligent officer." Perry was a determined expansionist who feared that the British—already in control of Hong Kong and Singapore trade—would soon control the entire region. He knew that the Dutch had managed to engage in limited trading with Japan, but only after making themselves totally subservient to their hosts. Similar attempts by an American captain seven years earlier had ended in humiliation. Perry would have none of that. In his official report, he insisted that rather than forfeit his dignity, he would "demand as a right, and not as a favor, those acts of courtesy which are due from one civilized nation to another."

On July 8, 1853, Perry steamed into Edo Bay, near Tokyo, with four ships spouting black smoke from their stacks. The ships carried 967 men and were mounted with sixty-one guns. The American warships, six times larger than any Japanese vessel, soon became known in Japanese lore as *kurofune*—"the black ships."

The fleet was quickly intercepted by several boats, rowed, according to the expedition's journals, "by tall, handsomely formed men... who, by their dress and the two swords stuck in their belts, appeared to be men of authority." In Japan, only the samurai wore two swords.

The Americans refused to communicate with these men, and even went so far as to drive them off with a "bristling array of pikes and cutlasses over the vessel's side that caused the Japanese to retreat in great haste."

The following morning, government officials approached the ships. After tentative talks,

Perry gave the officials a letter from President Fillmore with the understanding that it would be delivered to the emperor. He also gave them a number of white flags, stating that they would be useful to the Japanese as flags of surrender if they should fail to meet his peaceful demands. Leaving them with that threat of war, and a pledge to return for a response from the emperor in one year, Perry departed.

He returned the following February, earlier than the Japanese expected. By this time, the Russians, too, had visited Japan seeking trade agreements. Understanding that it no longer would be possible to remain isolated in a changing world, Japan signed a commercial treaty, the Treaty of Kanagawa, with the United States in 1854. Within six months, the island nation had similar agreements with Britain, France, Russia, and the Netherlands. For the first time in over 250 years, Japan's shores were open to international trade.

EXT. PARADE GROUND - NEXT DAY

BAGLEY
Nathan.
(takes Algren aside)
Katsumoto has attacked the railroad
at the border of his province.

Algren looks at the soldiers continuing to take
target practice.

OMURA
We cannot govern a country in which
we cannot travel freely…He must be
stopped now. My railroad is a priority
for this country.

ALGREN
They're not ready.

BAGLEY
The rebels don't have a single rifle.
They're savages with bows and arrows.

ALGREN
-- whose sole occupation for the last
thousand years has been war.

EXT. MOUNTAINS - DAY

The Imperial Army marches through the mountain landscape.

EXT. RUINED VILLAGE - DAY

GRAHAM
A thousand miles of rail track laid in
less than two years. It's astonishing.

ALGREN
And Omura owns all of it?

GRAHAM
As soon as he can get rid of the
samurai…well, yes.

武士
道

SAIGO TAKAMORI
AND THE SATSUMA REBELLION

*"Even with his head cut off, the samurai
must continue to attack."*

Yamamoto Tsunetomo
The Hagakure: The Book of the Samurai 1716

Saigo Takamori, the warrior who inspired
the character of Katsumoto, is one of the
most revered heroes of Japanese history.
Referred to as *Dai Saigo*—"Saigo the Great"—
the samurai is best remembered for his
participation in "restoring" Emperor Meiji
to power, and his later rebellion against that
same Imperial Court.

Saigo was born in 1827, in Satsuma, a
province marked by both its isolation behind
rugged mountains and its enduring rivalries
with the power centers in Kyoto and Tokyo.
The people of Satsuma celebrated their
separateness, and even emphasized it, by
fostering a dialect that was nearly incompre-
hensible to other Japanese.

During Saigo's childhood, there was
widespread unemployment among the
nation's samurai, and the atmosphere was
ripe for rebellion, with all anger aimed at
the *Bakufu,* the ruling *shogun* government
in Tokyo.

In 1868, opposition to the shogunate
came to a head, and Saigo led four
thousand loyalist warriors against twenty
thousand shogunate troops and trounced
them soundly. Fifteen-year-old Emperor
Meiji was restored to the throne. But while
Saigo's efforts earned him an Imperial
appointment to the post of commander-in-
chief of the armed services, court officials
worried about his popularity, and kept a
close watch on his activities.

Saigo had hoped the new government
would return to traditional values, but the
court recognized that progress was necessary
for the survival of Japan and continued to

adopt Western ways. The conservative Saigo
came to resent the Meiji regime that he'd
helped restore to power. He angrily informed
the emperor that he never again would
perform public service, and he retired to
Satsuma. As new laws, such as the anti-sword
edict, were passed, samurai throughout
Japan grew increasingly incensed.

Worried that Saigo may be instigating
this unrest, the government secretly sent
guns and other weapons to Satsuma in the
event that they might be needed to quell
an actual revolt. After a group of Saigo's
students discovered the cache of weapons,
a battle broke out. To Saigo, this was the
final insult, and he accepted the task of

leading an army against the very regime he had helped to put into power only a few years earlier.

The government was prepared for the insurrection. It sent sixty thousand men toward Satsuma, armed with Western weapons. Saigo and his army of disenfranchised samurai numbered only twenty thousand. The deadly struggle, dubbed the Satsuma Rebellion, continued for seven months. Finally, only Saigo and a few hundred of his samurai remained alive.

On September 24, 1877, government forces attacked the cave where the popular hero was camped. Saigo was hit with a single bullet. Unable to continue, he opened his own belly with his short sword. His friend, Beppu Shensuki, quickly beheaded the dying man.

But followers of Saigo Takamori refused to allow his name and reputation to die. His memory was so venerated by the Japanese citizenry that Emperor Meiji found it politically expedient to issue Saigo a pardon and a posthumous ranking among the court hierarchy. Images of the man and his exploits soon were being re-created in countless woodcuts, and a life-size statue was installed in Tokyo's Ueno Park. Today, over a century after his death, *Dai Saigo*'s presence continues to exist as a symbol of devotion to one's principles.

EXT. MOUNTAIN FOREST - MORNING

A thick fog. Everything is creepy.
Imminent. Algren is in motion,
barking orders as he rides the line...

A DISTANT RUMBLE of HORSES, building
through the fog, breaks the moment.
Then the sound of DRUMS. The Japanese
soldiers are literally shaking in fear.

武士道

EXT. MOUNTAIN FOREST - MORNING

Algren is surrounded by samurai. A man's heroic stand against certain death is of great interest to them. As they begin to close in, Algren whirls the lance, a tattered battle-flag with TIGER INSIGNIA still dangling from the end.

Katsumoto's eyes widen in surprise, he watches his dream come to life -- the white tiger holding the men at bay.

武
士
道

SEPPUKU: THE RITUAL OF HONORABLE SUICIDE

The act of *seppuku*—literally "self-disembowelment"—began in the twelfth century. A defeated samurai would preserve his dignity by disemboweling himself with his own sword rather than be taken captive after losing a battle. The samurai considered this to be a way of meeting death without disgrace or dishonor. The sword was a warrior's most treasured possession, and the abdomen was seen as the part of the body where a man's soul dwelled. Thus, the act of *seppuku* was seen as a way of setting his soul free.

of beheading the samurai himself and taking his head as a trophy.

During the peaceful Tokugawa period, *seppuku* developed into a fine art. A loyal warrior might follow the death of his master by taking his own life. A samurai who had been "shamed" by committing an act against his lord, or who was convicted of a criminal act, could choose to die by his own hand, thus erasing the disgrace of his deed and allowing his sons to inherit his name, position, and property. These acts of *seppuku* would be performed in a carefully prepared room, like a Buddhist temple or a garden where white sand had been sprinkled (white being the color of death). The condemned man would bathe and dress in a white kimono before entering the room. Kneeling on a pillow, with his trusted friend on his left and his *tanto*, or dagger, resting on a tray before him, he would open his robe to the waist, lift the sword and stab himself on the left side. Then he would draw the sword across to the right before making a slight upward cut. Carried out to its finish, this movement was known as a *jumonji*, or "crosswise cut." Quite often a samurai was unable to endure the entire procedure, however, prompting his friend to jump up at the first sign of pain and decapitate the impaled man.

Officially sanctioned and obligatory *seppuku* was banned in 1868, following the Meiji Restoration. In spite of this, on the day of Emperor Meiji's funeral, in 1912, Third Army Commander General Nogi and his wife joined their master in death.

The term *harakiri*, or "belly cutting," is a vulgar term popularly used only by Westerners, and never by the samurai.

In time, a *kaishaku*, or "second," assisted in the suicide by decapitating the dying warrior. The decapitation served two purposes: it was merciful, since slitting the belly open was a slow and painful way to die—and a samurai wished never to show pain—and it precluded allowing an enemy the privilege

武士道

WILL YOURSELF TO STAND READY
AND COURAGEOUS ON THE BATTLEFIELD.
IN THIS WAY, ALL THAT IS DIFFICULT
OR DANGEROUS WILL BE YOURS.

THE WAY OF THE SAMURAI

EXT. VILLAGE - DUSK

> **KATSUMOTO**
> What is your name?

Algren looks at him and refuses to answer.

Ujio races forward and SCREAMS at Algren
in Japanese...

> **UJIO**
> (subtitles)
> You insolent swine, answer!

Algren doesn't move. Ujio paces back and forth like
a caged panther spitting invective at Algren.

Algren doesn't move. He watches Ujio evenly.
This takes incredible will.

SUDDENLY -- Ujio draws his long sword --
it slashes through the air -- the blade singing -- and
stops an inch away from Algren's face!

Algren doesn't move.

Ujio brings the cutting edge into contact with
Algren's cheek. Blood runs where even this feather-
light touch cuts Algren's skin. Algren doesn't move.

Katsumoto speaks.

> **KATSUMOTO**
> (subtitles)
> Leave him be.

Ujio sheathes his sword and walks away. Katsumoto
looks at Algren deeply, gauging him.

> **KATSUMOTO**
> This is my son's village. We are deep in
> the mountains and the winter is coming.
> You cannot escape.

Katsumoto walks away. Nobutada smiles at him.

> **NOBUTADA**
> (proud of his only English)

47

武
士
道

TOM CRUISE ON THE PRODUCTION

"Ed Zwick is a personal filmmaker who makes epic films. Epic movies build on each moment, one moment at a time. Not one landscape at a time, but one moment at a time. And Ed wants that texture. He wants that reality. He wants that emotional journey.

"That's how I worked on my character. When I start feeling things about a character, I don't want to feel them intellectually, I want to feel them in my bones, and in my muscles. I want them in my behavior. I know where the story is going in the end, but I want the character to discover it. From his director's point of view, Ed is looking at the story. As an actor, I'm playing each scene, one at a time. Each scene adds to the structure of the story, but also to the overall structure of the character. I want to be surprised in each scene, just as my character is surprised. After I do my homework, I don't want it to be analytical anymore. I want it to be experiential.

"I want my director to direct me, and I had a blast working with Ed. He has wonderful insight into the characters, and he has such humanity. You could just see how he was hooked into this story. It was his. He owned it. He was born to direct this movie, and I felt very fortunate that he shared it with me.

"I've always wanted to make a movie of this nature. I've been a huge admirer of Kurosawa and samurai movies, and there's never been a samurai movie of this scale made in the West. *Bushido*, the code of the samurai, is what hooked me. Samurai philosophy, in its purity, offers great things to aspire to, even in this modern world. Things like, 'What is honor?' or concepts like, 'When you say you're going to do something, it's already done.' That level of responsibility and integrity are very close to me, very strong to my sensibility. I have a huge affinity for *Bushido*.

"The Japanese cast was just so extraordinary, so generous. They helped me with their language and encouraged me with the swords. They also helped me to feel confident in the customs, dress, language, and mannerisms that my character learns. Though never once did I feel that we had a language barrier while we were acting together.

"Everyday, Ed and I were high-fiving each other, so excited about what they were doing with their characters. Ken (Watanabe) gave such depth and dignity to Katsumoto that you can feel his spirituality and the weight and responsibility that the character is carrying for his people. For his heritage. For his ancestors.

"Hiro (Sanada) is a very powerful actor. Without benefit of many words, you can see the complex levels he gave to Ujio—and he was incredible at swinging a sword at my head without injuring me!

"Koyuki (Kato) couldn't speak English at all, but her characterization of Taka is very compelling. She always went beyond what had been discussed, and by the end of shooting, Ed and I would laugh and wonder, 'Do you think she knows more English than she's letting on?'

"*The Last Samurai* was an incredibly ambitious project. We shot on three continents. No matter how many movies we had all made, I don't think we could have anticipated the experience. Sometimes you don't know what you're doing until you're doing it. When we had finished shooting, we all sat down and said, 'Man, this was really something, wasn't it?'"

Paula Wagner and Edward Zwick

INT. TAKA'S HOUSE - NIGHT

Algren's eyes open…

A WOMAN is leaning close, her eyes intent
on the task of sewing up his wound. She is
beautiful, but he is not really conscious
enough to notice, or even feel the pain.
He blacks out again.

51

INT. TAKA'S HOUSE - PORCH - DAY

Algren...[is]...convulsed with shivering.
His withdrawal from alcohol, his isolation
and his imagined sins are devouring him.

FLASHBACK - THE WASHITA RIVER

The line of cavalry descends on the sleeping village.

In the distance, the first shots are fired, and the pandemonium of slaughter that slowly engulfs the village can only be seen from afar.

Algren takes a grim breath, then, as if his body weighs a thousand pounds, joins the attack.

武士道

53

THE INDIAN MASSACRES IN NATHAN ALGREN'S BACKSTORY

"Algren's disillusionment harkens back to an Indian massacre he participated in several years before our story starts," notes Marshall Herskovitz. "We based the idea on two actual massacres. One was at Sand Creek in Colorado, the other one, which involved the same Indians, was at the Washita River in Oklahoma."

The Sand Creek massacre took place on November 28, 1864, when the cavalry, under Colonel John M. Covington, attacked a band of Cheyenne Indians led by Chief Black Kettle. Only two months earlier, Black Kettle had met with Colorado Governor John Evans and Colonel Covington to discuss peace. During the negotiations, Black Kettle was given an American flag. Feeling that progress had been made, the Indians turned in their weapons and retired to their camp at the edge of the reservation.

When Black Kettle saw the cavalry approaching on the morning of the attack, he raised the American flag, along with a white flag. Regardless, the troops attacked, killing about 150 men, women, and children, and mutilating their bodies. The following January, the House of Representatives officially condemned Covington's actions as a "gross and wanton outrage." Black Kettle survived, and was granted a parcel of land in reparation.

Four years later almost to the day, on November 27, 1868, Black Kettle's band of Plains Indians was camped on the Washita River in Indian Territory, which later would become Oklahoma. Only five days earlier, Black Kettle had gone to Fort Cobb to surrender. Colonel W. B. Hazen, the man in charge at the time, insisted that only General Philip Sheridan could negotiate peace with the Indians. The next day, Sheridan was told of Black Kettle's offer, but rather than meet with the chief, Sheridan ordered the 7th Cavalry, led by General George Armstrong Custer, to destroy the Indians.

The morning of the massacre, four columns of troops surrounded the camp. "The Indians were caught napping for once," Custer wrote in his report to Sheridan. "There never was a more complete surprise. My men charged the village, and reached the lodges before the Indians were aware of our presence." As the soldiers were attacking, Black Kettle and his wife Medicine Woman walked into the open with their arms raised, but they were shot instantly. The soldiers quickly killed 150 men, women, and children, and then spent several hours destroying over 800 Indian ponies and mules.

Several days later at Fort Cobb, Custer bragged about his success at Washita, not knowing that five years later he would face another Indian gathering—in Montana, at the Little Big Horn.

55

武士道

EXT. VILLAGE - DAY

Algren walks through the village, his guard following at a respectful distance.

This is the first time he really sees the splendor of the setting, and the simple beauty of village life…

On a nearby hillside, the samurai train. Algren watches. Part sacred ritual, part martial preparation, they combine athletic prowess and graceful artistry into one effortless whole.

Kendo ("The Way of the Sword") masters practice with their wooden swords…

Kyudo ("The Way of the Bow") masters use their bows for target practice…

INT. SMALL ROOM - DAY

Algren opens a sliding shoji screen and discovers a small room that has been made into a shrine. Candles and incense burn but Algren's eyes are drawn to what seems like an apparition standing in the corner.

The BRIGHT RED ARMOR of the warrior Algren killed in the fog is held upright by an unseen stand. It is almost as if the dead warrior himself is staring back at him…

EXT. KATSUMOTO'S COMPOUND - DAY

> ALGREN
> I have questions.

Katsumoto stops and turns back to Algren.

> KATSUMOTO
> Questions come later.

> ALGREN
> Who was the warrior in the
> red armor?

Katsumoto stops, considers, relents.

> KATSUMOTO
> My brother-in-law. Hirotaro.

> ALGREN
> And the woman who cares for me?

> KATSUMOTO
> My sister, Hirotaro's wife. Her name
> is Taka.

> ALGREN
> (incredulous)
> I killed her husband?

> KATSUMOTO
> It was a good death.

59

BUSHIDO:
THE WAY OF THE WARRIOR

*"The way of the samurai is often found in death.
When it comes to the alternatives of life or death,
there is only the quick choice of death.
This is not particularly difficult—
Be resolved and charge forward."*

Yamamoto Tsunetomo
The Hagakure: The Book of the Samurai, 1716

Bushido, or "the Way of the Warrior," is a
code of conduct, ethics, and honor that
developed among the samurai over many
centuries. The code emphasized discipline
and austerity, and demanded unwavering
loyalty (*go-on to hoko,* "obligations and
service") to a samurai's *daimyo,* or overlord.

The very heart of *Bushido* is expressed in
the first, and most famous, of 1,300 aphorisms
assembled in a book, *The Hagakure* (literally,
"Hidden in the Leaves"), that was published
in 1716. "The way of the samurai is found in
death," begins the text. But that "rule" is not
an instruction for the reader to seek death.
The text goes on to explain that once a warrior
is steeled to the *fact* of his dying, he may then
live his life without worrying *about* dying.

The constant themes in the samurai code
are death and loyalty to one's master: "One
who determines to live only for today, and take
no thought of tomorrow, must stand before
his lord thinking of it as his last appearance,"

it says. "Only then will his duty, his love of life, and his regard for his lord be sincere."

Bushido directed the warrior to set aside such distractions as self-pride or the desire to waste time or energy with the mundane. "Eliminate the unnecessary" may have been the unspoken battle cry in his mind. All thought became thought of militant service to his overlord, until even the distraction of thought itself was lifted away. The Zen perfection of "free-mindedness," or "no mind" came into play. With freedom from distraction a fact of his existence, the samurai was emancipated to pursue perfection in all things, from *haiku* to *seppuku*. And by reaching perfection in all he endeavored, including *kendo*, the Way of the Sword, he became an unbeatable warrior.

"Only when you train your spirit and your body each day to such an extent that there are none comparable to you among your fellow samurai, will it be possible for you to defeat your enemy."

That is *Bushido*. That is the way of the warrior. For the samurai, it was the way of life.

武
士
道

61

EXT. VILLAGE - DAY - RAINING

Suddenly, everyone goes silent. Higen backs away. Algren turns.

Ujio is standing behind him, wooden sword in hand.

It's obvious to Algren what he must mean, but Algren does nothing…

Ujio's wooden sword FLASHES, quicker than the eye can follow. Algren's sword is knocked from his hands, then, somehow in the same fluid movement, Ujio brings the sword around and cracks Algren across the chest hard enough to knock the breath from his body and send him to his knees…

Satisfied with himself, Ujio walks away, but the expressions of the bystanders cause him to turn back: Algren is standing again, holding the sword.

Nearby, Taka watches with interest. There is some atavistic satisfaction in seeing Algren physically punished.

Higen also watches closely.

武士道

The Silent Samurai merely stares at Algren as Ujio spin-kicks him in the stomach, followed by a blow to the shin. Algren is swept off his feet facedown in the mud…

The ever-enlarging crowd gasps as Algren once again struggles to get up, swiping his sword at Ujio…

Ujio delivers the final blows upon Algren's now defenseless body. First the shoulder, then finally the head.

Something begins to change in Taka's regard. Her appetite for vengeance is not as great as she might have imagined. Higen, too, finds himself reluctantly impressed by Algren's determination.

武
士
道

武
士
道

EXT. KATSUMOTO'S COMPOUND - DAY

KATSUMOTO
You were the general of your army?

ALGREN
No. I was a captain.

KATSUMOTO
This is a low rank?

ALGREN
A middle rank.

KATSUMOTO
Who was your general?

ALGREN
Don't you have a rebellion to lead?

KATSUMOTO
People in your country do not like
conversation?

ALGREN
He was a lieutenant colonel…his
name was Custer.

KATSUMOTO
I know this name. He killed many
warriors.

ALGREN
Ah, yes. Many warriors.

KATSUMOTO
So, he was a good general.

ALGREN
No. No, he wasn't a good general.
He was arrogant and foolhardy, and
he got massacred because he took a
single battalion against two thousand
angry Indians.

KATSUMOTO
Two thousand Indians? How many
men for Custer?

ALGREN
Two hundred and eleven.

KATSUMOTO
I like this General Custer.

ALGREN
He was a murderer who fell in love
with his own legend and his troopers
died for it.

KATSUMOTO
I think this is a very good death.

ALGREN
Well, maybe you can have one just like
it some day.

ALGREN (V.O.)
1876, day unknown, month unknown.
I continue to live among these unusual
people…I am their captive in that I
cannot escape. Mostly I'm treated with
a kind of a mild neglect, as if I were a
stray dog, or an unwelcome guest.
Everyone is polite. Everyone smiles
and bows, but beneath their courtesy
I detect a deep reservoir of feeling.

They are an intriguing people. From
the moment they wake, they devote
themselves to the perfection of
whatever they pursue -- I have never
seen such discipline…

武士道

ZEN, SWORDSMANSHIP, AND THE TEA CEREMONY

"The underpinnings of how the samurai lived owes much to Zen," Marshall Herskovitz says. "They embraced the fact that life is ephemeral, that death is as important as life, and that finally all you have is the moment you're in right now. We wanted to make the movie as much about that philosophy as about the samurai themselves. So it's filled with ideas of what life is about, how one lives one's life, and what it means to be an honorable person."

Zen, a meditative Buddhist sect, seems an unlikely source of inspiration for warriors. Nonetheless, it is Zen that inspired the samurai more than any other ideology. When paired with the rigorous mental and physical principles of swordsmanship, Zen teachings melded seamlessly into the samurai philosophy of *Bushido*. Ironically, that melding was successful, in part, because of a definitively gentle exercise: the tea ceremony.

In the year 1191, a Buddhist monk named Eisai returned home from a religious pilgrimage to China. During his trip, he had become intrigued by an independent school of Buddhism, *Ch'an*, or Zen, which practiced meditation as a means of reaching "enlightenment."

Eisai hoped to establish a Zen temple in Kyoto, near the Imperial Court. He was surprised, however, to discover that since his departure the Japanese government had been overturned and the Imperial court no longer ruled. Governing power had been usurped by the warrior class, and the first *shogun* had established a new government.

When the court in Kyoto showed no interest in his new teachings, Eisai took his message to the shogunate, where he not only was accepted, but also was invited to build his temple.

Zen's appeal to the warrior class was twofold. First, its philosophical concepts were distinctly different from the traditional religious teachings espoused by the imperial court, thereby emphasizing the samurai's unique identity and independence. Second, and more important,

it introduced to the samurai the all-important practice of meditation.

The two focuses of the samurai's calling— unfailing loyalty to one's lord and the constant preparation for death—required intense mental and spiritual training. Meditation proved to be the perfect conduit for that training. By meditating, the warrior discovered that he could eradicate all distraction from his mind and reach a state of "no mind," or "belly-wisdom."

The samurai also discovered, to their dismay, that meditation could be the perfect conduit for falling asleep. It was Eisai who hit upon the antidote: the drinking of tea. He devised a simple method of stirring powdered *matcha*—green tea leaves—into boiling water and then whipping the mixture with a *chasen*, or bamboo whisk, until it formed a light foam. Not only did the tea keep the drinker vigilant in his meditation, but the ritual of brewing it—a combination of delicate utensils,

simple activities, and soothing sounds—elevated his frame of mind to the spiritual level he required in order to perform flawlessly on the battlefield.

Eisai's tea-drinking ritual spread throughout Japan's warrior class quickly. Within fifty years, it had been refined into an art form known as *cha-no-you*, or the "tea ceremony." And within generations, the artistry of the tea ceremony had influenced every aspect of Japanese life, from architecture to calligraphy to flower arranging.

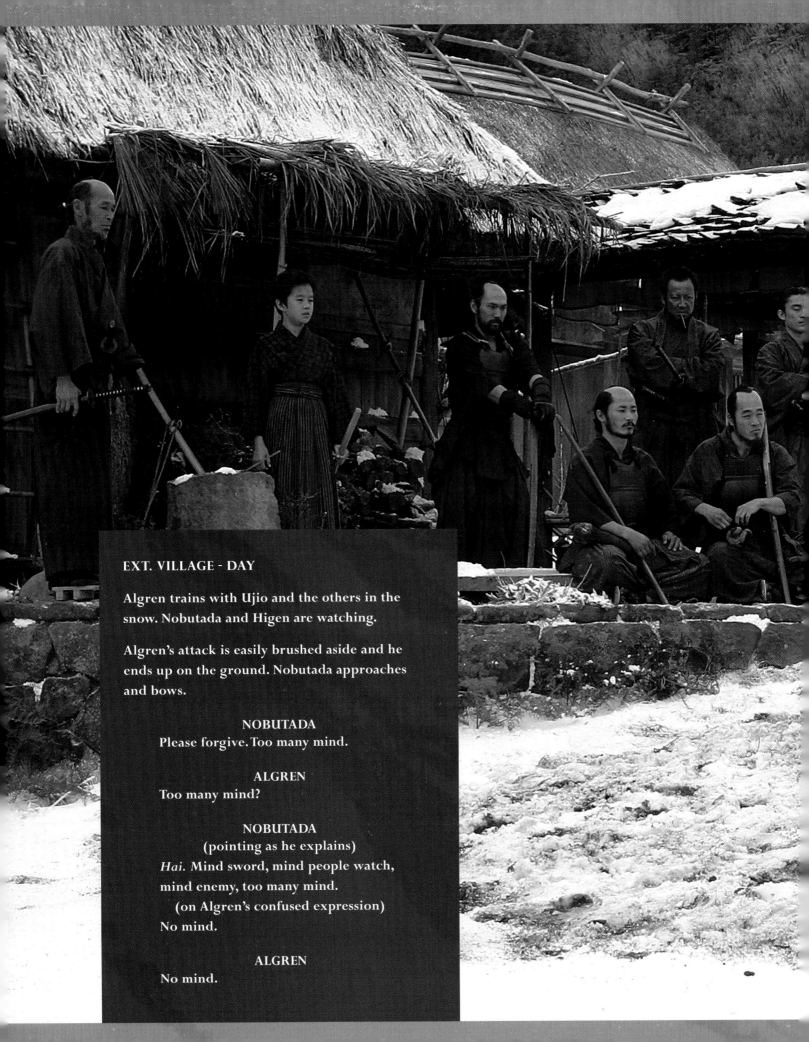

EXT. VILLAGE - DAY

Algren trains with Ujio and the others in the snow. Nobutada and Higen are watching.

Algren's attack is easily brushed aside and he ends up on the ground. Nobutada approaches and bows.

NOBUTADA
Please forgive. Too many mind.

ALGREN
Too many mind?

NOBUTADA
(pointing as he explains)
Hai. Mind sword, mind people watch, mind enemy, too many mind.
(on Algren's confused expression)
No mind.

ALGREN
No mind.

EXT. TAKA'S HOUSE - DAY

TAKA
(subtitles)
Brother please make him leave,
I cannot stand it.

KATSUMOTO
(subtitles)
Is he so repulsive?

TAKA
(subtitles)
The shame is unbearable. I ask
permission to end my life.

KATSUMOTO
(subtitles)
You will do as you are told! Would
you rather I kill him to avenge your
husband?

TAKA
(subtitles)
…Yes.

KATSUMOTO
(subtitles)
Hirotaro tried to kill the American.
It was Karma.

TAKA
(subtitles)
I know. Forgive my weakness.

KATSUMOTO
(softens his tone;
subtitles)
There must be some reason why he's
here.
(beat)
It's beyond my understanding.

GIVING LIFE TO NATHAN ALGREN

"Ed Zwick and I get along famously." John Logan laughs. "But we have completely different ways of looking at the world. Ed is contemplative. Ed has a sort of Zen philosophy on life. Me, I'm more in the vein of, 'Let's *do* something! Let's work this thing!'

"While we were writing the scenes of Algren in the village," he explains, "Ed would say quietly, 'The character has to witness things around him. He's injured, so he can't move, and he witnesses the cherry blossom change.' And I'd go, 'Yeah! But then he has to get a sword! He has to see how a Japanese sword feels compared to an American Cavalry sword!' Between us, we found the two sides of the character.

John Logan

"We ended up with sweeping battles, and all the swashbuckling panache anyone would want in a big adventure movie," Logan adds enthusiastically. "But being that it's an Ed Zwick movie, it has a moral center, even a theological center. It deals with the very turbulent waters of Algren's soul."

Probing the depths of those waters became the focus for the filmmakers. "We wanted the character to be a wounded animal," Logan says. "He's tormented by grief because of what he's seen, and because he's always been a soldier, he's completely lacking a sense of self. But after being taken into Katsumoto's world, he goes through a long process of assimilation, and reaches a crossroads where he has to ask himself, 'Who am I?'"

"Algren is thrust into a new world," says producer Paula Wagner, "where he has an epiphany of sorts. It's a dynamic emotional, intellectual, spiritual, and personal journey."

"Constructing the relationship between Algren and Katsumoto was the biggest risk that we took with the script," producer Marshall Herskovitz says. "Creating long conversations in the middle of an action movie means taking a chance. But we knew it was the heart of the story, so we couldn't take a short cut."

Zwick says the script "rose to the next level" when Tom Cruise began to contribute to the character of Algren. "There's a point where a character just reveals himself to you," says Cruise. "At the beginning of the Civil War, he was a guy who felt he was fighting on the right side—for the freedom of man. But then he went to fight for the Seventh Cavalry, under Custer. The authorities told him that every man was free but that the Indians weren't men. That's when his disillusionment began."

"Tom was interested in exploring active means of portraying Algren's torment," says Zwick. He found ways to dramatize qualities that might not otherwise have "risen off the page." Herskovitz adds, "Tom embraced the idea that you don't love Algren because of the way he turns a phrase, you just see that he's a very strong man who has gone through a lot."

"The world well knows Tom's gifts, his energy, his charm and his intensity. But what I have always sensed is the emotional complexity and soulfulness of his inner life," says Zwick. "Tom's performance is deeply internal. I think, to some, it will be a revelation."

With his character's motivation solidified, Cruise decided to grow a beard and let his hair grow long. Herskovitz says, "It made him look older. Then our incredible makeup artist, Lois Burwell, transformed him in subtle ways. She emphasized the lines in his face and the shadows under his cheeks so you would look at him and say, 'Oh yeah, that's a guy who's seen battles and death.' Lois took this beautiful man and messed him up every morning," Herskovitz says. "That's the character," Cruise says, laughing. "Whatever's right for the character."

武
士
道

ALGREN (V.O.)
Spring, 1877. This marks the longest
I have stayed in one place since I left
the farm at seventeen...

There is so much here that I will
never understand...

I have never been a church-going
man. And what I have seen on the
field of battle has led me to question
God's purpose.

ALGREN (V.O.)
But there is indeed something spiritual
in this place. And though it may forever
be obscure to me, I cannot but be aware
of its power.

EXT. VILLAGE - NIGHT

The entire village has gathered to celebrate
spring planting. Torches illuminate a small stage
near Taka's house, where actors perform *Kyogen*, a
comic form...

Algren sits back and takes in the fullness of
the moment...

[H]e notices something odd -- a blackness darker
than the sky, the slightest shifting of a shadow on
a rooftop.

His eyes return to the stage, but something
nags at him, and he quickly realizes what it is:
the guards are now gone...

He jumps to his feet --

              ALGREN
       KATSUMOTO!

...Katsumoto turns at the sound of Algren's voice,
and this act saves his life -- as a crossbow BOLT
WHISTLES past where his head just was, into the
mask of the actor behind him --

Villagers scream as --

Arrows and throwing stars rain down on the
unprotected square --

武
士
道

TRAINING:
FROM ACTOR TO WARRIOR

"We were very lucky on this film to have someone as committed and able as Tom Cruise," says stunt coordinator Nick Powell. "Without a doubt, he is the most determined professional sort of athletic actor that I've ever worked with."

"The story of Algren's training in the movie is also the story of Tom's training," explains Ed Zwick. "I don't think there was a day when Tom didn't work for hours, just so he could reach a level of proficiency that would allow him to compete with Hiro Sanada and Ken Watanabe, who had been handling swords their whole lives."

Tom Cruise's transformation from actor to warrior didn't happen overnight. "Nick Powell trained me from zero up, every step of the

way," acknowledges Cruise. "I didn't know how to do any of that stuff. I worked on my flexibility, and I had to change my body. I ended up putting on about eighteen pounds of muscle for the character, because the armor was very heavy."

"We worked on all the basics," says Powell. "All the two-handed sword work, all the different cuts, all the parries, all the footwork. The footwork is very complicated. You need good balance and a low center of gravity. We used some of the footwork from formal *kendo*, with one foot forward, sort of like boxing. But *kendo* is very modern, so to get more of a period feel we also used footwork from *aikido* and *jujitsu*, always keeping the balance and never crossing the feet.

"We started by training Tom with wooden swords, but we ended up having him use the steel, so that he got the feel of a real sword," Powell explains. "Once he had mastered the basics, we went on to more advanced maneuvers, until finally Tom was spinning two swords in different directions, with both hands at the same time, very fluidly and fluently."

"Nick prepared me so well that we could ad-lib on the day of shooting," says Cruise. "That way, Ed could change a routine and I could respond with several moves and Nick knew that I would be safe. Because you had wooden swords coming at your head, you had metal coming at your head. But he got me to the point where I wasn't concerned about it. I was in the fight. I had the immediacy of knowing what my next three moves were and predicting what the other guy was going to do."

Learning not to flinch proved to be a crucial part of Cruise's training. "There's a scene that takes place in the samurai village, where Ujio beats up Algren because Algren won't drop his sword," says Zwick. "The script called for Hiroyuki Sanada to hit Tom Cruise in the face, in the neck and in the stomach." Powell adds,

"We started out thinking we should do it with multiple passes, but then Hiro said, 'Oh, no, I can just bring the sword right up to his face and not hit him.' And I thought, 'No, no, we can't risk hitting Tom in the nose.'" Powell laughs at the memory. "We had decided to shoot the scene in the rain, and Tom and Hiro were soaking wet. There are shots in the movie where, head on, you see that sword come right to Tom's nose, and you see Tom's head snap back, and you cannot believe that Hiro didn't hit him. But in fact, he just brought the sword up to within a millimeter of Tom's nose and then Tom jerked his head back. It looks like a brutal, bone-breaking hit. We did five different hits just like it, take after take for the different camera angles. In the mud. In the pouring rain."

Powell's favorite fight sequence is the attack on Algren by four *ronin* on a deserted Tokyo street. "Normally in a film, when four guys with swords come at someone, one guy attacks, then the next guy attacks, then the next," Powell relates. "But Ed and I wanted to see what it would really be like if four people tried to attack at the same time, and how the protagonist would get out of that. I choreographed it very early and we spent three months working on it."

"It was very complex," Cruise recalls. "And we shot it all in one take. Normally, when you're doing stunts, you'll do one shot, and then you'll reset, and then another shot, and the audience will see those cuts in the movie. But we did that sequence of stunts right from beginning to end. It was a lot of fun."

Zwick is rightfully proud of his lead actor. "I remember the first time Tom held a katana, trying to get the feel of it," the director says. "Seeing how far he's come is pretty great."

Cruise laughs as he reflects on the experience. "I started out knowing nothing about this. Now you see those fight sequences in the film, and I think, who did that?"

武
士
道

THE SOUL IS THE BODY,
AND THE BODY IS THE SOUL.
THEY ARE INDISTINGUISHABLE.
DO NOT FEAR FOR THE
DESTRUCTION OF EITHER.
THE WAY OF THE SAMURAI

EXT. KATSUMOTO'S COMPOUND - DAY

KATSUMOTO (O.S.)
A perfect blossom is a rare thing… You
could spend your life looking for one.
And it would not be a wasted life.

ALGREN
Who sent those men to kill you?

KATSUMOTO
I am writing a poem about a dream I
had. The tiger's eyes are like my own.
But he comes from across a deep and
troubled sea.

ALGREN
Was it the emperor? Omura?

KATSUMOTO
If the emperor wishes my death, he has
but to ask.

ALGREN
So it was Omura.

Katsumoto calls out an order in Japanese. A servant
runs to do his bidding.

KATSUMOTO
You have seen many things.

ALGREN
I have.

KATSUMOTO
And you do not fear death.
(looks at him)
But sometimes you wish for it. Is this
not so?

Algren doesn't answer right away. Katsumoto has
intuited a dark truth.

ALGREN
Yes.

KATSUMOTO
I, also. It happens to men
who have seen what we have seen.
(looks around)
And then I come to this place of my
ancestors. And I remember… like these
blossoms, we are all dying.
(looks back at him)
To know life in every breath. Every
cup of tea. Every life we take. The way
of the warrior.

He takes in the beautiful orchard.

ALGREN
Life in every breath.

KATSUMOTO
That is Bushido.

武
士
道

武士道
90

EXT. ROTENBURO BATHS - DAY

Algren arrives. For a moment he watches Taka in
the midst of washing her hair.

She wears only a silken gown, and he cannot help
but notice the beauty of her bare arms. He watches
for a long moment before she is aware of him…

> ALGREN
> (subtitles)
>
> I must go away.

> TAKA
>
> *Hai.*

She wraps her hair in a towel, and starts to walk
past him.

She stops. They are standing very close together.

> ALGREN
> (subtitles)
>
> You have been kind to me.
> (she cannot answer)
> I won't forget…

Her eyes are unguarded for just a moment.
And for once, he can see that her feelings for him
are deep and complex. Then she is gone.

91

FINDING THE RIGHT ACTORS

"The process of casting is a bit like having wishes," says Marshall Herskovitz. "You think, 'Oh, I wish I could work with that person.' You go through name after name as you try to bend your mind and think of who could be great in a part."

The filmmakers had a very specific wish for the actor who would portray their protagonist. "It didn't take a genius to know that we'd need a major star to play Algren." Ed Zwick laughs. "Tom Cruise was a dream choice."

The director and Cruise had met "many years before," and they had talked about working together in the intervening years, but had never found the right project. Zwick instinctively knew that *The Last Samurai* finally presented an opportunity for the two of them.

At Zwick's invitation, Cruise read the script. Then the two men met to talk about the project. "Ed showed me photographs of what he wanted the film to look like," Cruise recalls. "And as he told me his ideas, he was jumping around the room like a sixteen-year-old kid. From his enthusiasm alone, I got hooked. And then I read the script and that was it."

"Tom had extraordinary ideas, not just about his character, but for the whole movie. We talked for days," Zwick says. "He is so experienced, and so respectful of the writing process, that we just seized on his ideas. He genuinely became our collaborator."

"We began with Ed's vision and started talking," says Cruise. "It was like a great game of half-court basketball where you're just feeding the ball to each other. We kept pushing ideas back and forth, working on the themes and the relationships. The ideas kept evolving and evolving. Then Marshall joined in and it just got better."

The next challenge was finding an actor to play the Japanese lead, Katsumoto. Zwick made a series of trips to Japan for casting

and location scouting purposes. "I saw many wonderful actors," he says, "but none measured up to the Katsumoto of my imagination. It wasn't until the eleventh hour that our Katsumoto walked in."

The actor was Ken Watanabe, who had starred in dozens of films in Japan, but who had never before acted in English. "It took all of two minutes for me to realize I was in the imposing presence of someone with the strength to play Katsumoto," Zwick says. "Of course, at the time, I had no way of knowing just how warm, intuitive, and inventive an actor he was."

"I didn't know what the script was about when I went in, but I wanted to meet the director," Watanabe recalls. "Edward made me very relaxed. It was the first time that I spoke English in a film, and it was difficult, because the Japanese—and especially the samurai—in Japanese movies, speak without changing their expression or attitude. But I like to act with a variety of Japanese dialects, so I tried to think of English as just another dialect as well."

93

Zwick was also excited to be able to cast Hiroyuki Sanada in the part of Ujio. "Hiro is one of the most formidable actors in Japan, and also one of its biggest stars," he says. "I had been impressed by his work for many years."

"Hiro is a leading man who can play anything from light comedy to Shakespeare. He even played the Fool in *King Lear* at The National Theatre in London," Herskovitz adds. " As it happens, Sanada also is an accomplished martial artist, so the role was perfect for him.

For the role of Katsumoto's sister, Taka, Zwick auditioned dozens of actresses before meeting Koyuki Kato. "Koyuki is a remarkable actress, and also very beautiful, but she alone captured the sophistication and sorrow of the character."

The fact that Koyuki spoke no English was not seen as an obstacle by the filmmakers. "Algren and Taka's relationship is a very unique love story," producer Paula Wagner explains. "They are people from two different worlds who make contact in very subtle ways—through looks and through gesture. As actors, emotion and intention don't always require words."

Zwick and Herskovitz still had to bring three major Western characters to life— Sergeant Zebulon Gant, Colonel Benjamin Bagley, and the English expatriate Simon Graham. "We had created Gant as sort of an homage to Victor McLaglen, the Scottish actor who had played an Irishman in all the John Ford movies," Herskovitz says. "And then we ended up casting Billy Connolly, who's a Scotsman, to play an Irishman."

"Ed told me about that," Billy Connolly says, chuckling, "and it's nice to be thought of in the same equation with Victor McLaglen. But I saw it differently. I saw that I got to play the happy, likeable guy who always dies first!"

For the character of Colonel Bagley, the film-makers wanted an actor who could invest the character with enough power and intelligence to make him a worthy nemesis for Algren. They chose Tony Goldwyn.

"Bagley is the villain," Tony Goldwyn says. "But I saw him as an empire builder with views that were very typically nineteenth-century American. Whether you like Bagley or you dislike him, he represents a very accurate point of view."

The third Western character is Simon Graham, who serves as translator to Algren. The role went to Timothy Spall, one of the most celebrated character actors in England. "Graham is a British misfit who ended up in Japan and adored the culture," says Spall. "He's an observer who loves to pass information along and has the unfortunate habit of telling the truth, so his function in the story is to inform the audience about the political situation. But it's not just for exposition—he does it out of his love for the country. He's quite an eccentric."

"In the end," Zwick notes, "casting always feels like something of a miracle. You can't believe there was ever more than one person to play any of the parts, and you were just fortunate enough to find them."

武士道

EXT. TOKYO STREET - DAY

Katsumoto, Algren and the samurai ride
down the middle of the street. People
scatter in their wake.

武士道

97

EXT. IMPERIAL PALACE WALKWAY - CONTINUOUS

KATSUMOTO
It is <u>your</u> voice we need, Highness. You are
a living god, you do what you think is
right.

EMPEROR
I am a living god as long as I do what <u>they</u>
think is right.

KATSUMOTO
What sad words you speak. Forgive me
for saying what a teacher must...have you
forgotten your people?

EMPEROR
Tell me what to do...my teacher.

KATSUMOTO
You are emperor, my lord, not me.
You must find the wisdom for all of us.

JAPAN'S IMPERIAL HERITAGE:
A LINE OF POWERLESS GODS

For most of Japan's history, the emperor reigned but did not rule.

In the year 660 B.C., Jimmu, allegedly a descendent of the Sun Goddess, founded the Imperial Dynasty and became the first emperor. Referred to by all as the *tenno*, or "heavenly prince," the emperor served as nominal ruler and the high priest of the primary religion, Shinto, while the court's aristocracy dominated Japan's political and cultural life.

Court nobles used their position to accumulate large tracts for themselves—and then, to protect their estates from rivals, they assembled large private armies, laying the seeds for the samurai class that would dominate Japan for the next 700 years. The landholders, known as *daimyo*, or "great lords," became extremely powerful, and the most powerful of them all was the *shogun*, or "supreme military commander."

Over the centuries, the lords continuously battled among themselves in bloody attempts to increase their domains. Then, in the seventeenth century, *shogun* Tokugawa Ieyasu finally succeeded in calming the society, and for the next 250 years, the samurai class turned to pursuits such as farming or administration, while retaining their *Bushido* philosophy.

Peace ultimately proved difficult for many of these warriors, and in 1868, discontented and poverty-stricken samurai spearheaded a military campaign against the *shogun* government that culminated in the fall of the Tokugawa regime. This successful campaign restored power to the emperor—or at least to the Imperial Court. As before, the powers of administration and justice lay in the hands of the *genro*—an elite group of court officials, advisors, and ex-samurai—rather than with the new *tenno*, the 15-year-old Emperor Meiji.

The new government set Japan on a path toward modernization. The officials abolished the ancient class system, redistributed land held by the *daimyo* lords, and—in an act aimed directly at the samurai—banned the wearing of swords in public. The long-standing feudal military system was finally dismantled and replaced with a national army.

The forward-looking leaders sent delegations abroad to study cultural, economic, and political techniques, and invited Western engineers, teachers, and scientists to visit Japan. Young Emperor Meiji put himself at the forefront of this modernization movement. He was among the first to wear Western clothing, and his followers quickly imitated his style. As emperor, Meiji's main occupation was to attend the dedications of bridges and railways, but he was far more passionate about introducing an obligatory school system to his country. In 1890, the Meiji Constitution was installed, establishing the legislative body known as the *Diet*.

Emperor Meiji served as a symbol of national unity and a source of legislative legitimacy throughout his lifetime. He succeeded in elevating Japan onto the world stage as well as affecting domestic social change.

INT. ALGREN'S QUARTERS - DAY

Algren is packing his few belongings, a half-drunk bottle of whiskey is nearby. The calligraphy scroll given him by Higen lays on the bed…

A KNOCK at the door. It is Bagley.

> BAGLEY
> Well, it is pretty much over.
> Katsumoto's under arrest. Omura
> won't let him last the night…With
> Katsumoto dead, we'll have little
> trouble handling what's left of the
> rebellion -- even without you.
> <u>Especially</u> without you…
>
> Just tell me one thing. What is it
> about your own people that you
> hate so much?

武士道

EXT. TOKYO STREET - NIGHT

Algren walks down a shadowy street, lit only by torches. He is being followed again, and he knows it...

Algren stops, looks behind him. The two followers are there. Algren is trapped.

The Ronin begin to close in.

Algren appears to close his eyes. And the sound of the approaching footsteps fades as we HEAR ONLY the sound of his breathing...

EXT. YOKOHAMA HARBOR - DUSK

Algren walks toward the ship. He stops, stands there. All he need do is walk up the gangplank and leave this troubled land behind. For years he has had no connection, not only to other people, but to the truest part of himself.

And yet that truest part had started to come to life in a little village high in the mountains of Japan...

A moment later he turns away from the ship. And starts back toward town.

武士道

Algren gently opens his eyes. Everything
has SLOWED DOWN: a sign in the breeze,
a piece of rubbish on the street, the flame
of a nearby torch.

A BLUR OF MOTION.

Everything happens so fast it is hard
to tell just what has taken place. In the
strobing shadows, all we really know is
that Algren has leapt to the attack.

Within seconds, four bodies lie
in the street.

Algren holds a bloody sword.

His face is cut, a sleeve is ripped,
but other than that he is unharmed.
Ujio has taught him well.

105

ALGREN
I decided to stay -- see if I could
convince you to escape.

EXT. KATSUMOTO'S HOUSE - NIGHT

…Nobutada leans against the trunk, sliding to the ground, gravely wounded. Blood flows from his mouth.

> **NOBUTADA**
> (subtitles)
> Father. Let me stay. It is my time.

Nobutada's determination is absolute… Katsumoto is being torn apart inside as his son bravely prepares to sacrifice himself.

> **UJIO**
> (subtitles)
> My lord…we must go.

Katsumoto pulls Nobutada to his feet. He looks at his son and then leaves, followed by Ujio. Nobutada bows to Algren who then also bows.

A beat. Nobutada closes his eyes.

Then he launches himself into the darkened bridge firing arrows until he has no more. He reaches for both his swords --

The guards FIRE.

He is HIT again and again, but still he comes, screaming, wading forward -- his sword flashing.

It is a glorious death.

And his sacrifice has bought the others the necessary time to race off into the darkness.

107

武士道

SETS AND LOCATIONS

"One of the reasons I love making movies is that I get to create places that don't exist anymore, except in our imagination," says director Edward Zwick. For *The Last Samurai,* the filmmakers wanted to "visit" historical Japan, specifically 1876 and 1877. And it was during one of their many location scouts to Japan that they heard about a thousand-year-old mountaintop temple that could be reached only by funicular. "We were told that it was particularly beautiful, but it wasn't clear whether we could get our equipment up there," says Zwick. "Something about that description intrigued us, so we decided to take a look. We went up that mountain on the funicular, and when Engyoji Temple emerged through the mist, it was one of the most awe-inspiring places that I've ever seen."

Engyoji Temple, on western Japan's Mt. Shosha, was built in the year 966 by a Tendai Buddhist monk named Shoku after he saw a "celestial being" sitting in a cherry tree at the site. Shoku carved a statue from the

tree, then built a temple around the statue. The temple has been active as a seminary ever since. To everyone's surprise, it had never been used as a film location.

Originally, Katsumoto's compound had played only a small part in the script. Engyoji Temple, Zwick says, "inspired us to incorporate it much more, both visually and narratively, into our story." What's more, the director adds, "We knew that it was where we should start shooting."

Everyone on the crew recognized what an honor it was to film in and around the monastery. "Out of respect, we had to take our shoes off in order to enter," Herskovitz says. "So we had a ninety-person crew, all in their stocking feet, on wonderful ancient wooden floors."

"Engyoji Temple was an incredible place to begin," says Zwick. "On that mountaintop, in that forest, in that remnant of old Japan, the spirituality was quite remarkable. On the first day of shooting, the monks blessed the production in a lovely ceremony. The privilege of starting the movie there infused the whole

武
士
道

production with a spirit I'm not sure we could have done without."

While the film crew was shooting in Japan, production designer Lilly Kilvert and her staff were busy in California, on the Warner Bros. backlot. Their task was to transform a famous permanent set known as "New York Street" into nineteenth-century Tokyo. "Building a set of this scale on the backlot was quite wonderful," Kilvert enthuses. "You don't get to do that very often." Kilvert calls herself "a big research nut." After collecting hundreds of books and thousands of photographs, she began to design an "authentic" set that would work for the camera. "Japanese architecture is extremely rigid in style," she says. "There is a reason for every architectural choice. It all has to do with a philosophy of simplicity and regularity and peacefulness. A tatami mat is exactly so wide, and a shoji screen is exactly so high. Each room has to be pitched just so. It's wonderful, but it's not quite pleasant to photograph, because what the camera picks up is different from what the eye picks up. So after

I did the research and understood the truth, I started to break the rules and go from historical authenticity to what 'feels' correct."

When the actors, director, and production crew arrived after ten days of shooting in Japan, the Tokyo set awaited them. "Lilly's sets had the right Japanese fabrics, the right Japanese building materials, and Japanese actors in the correct garb," says Herskovitz. "We photographed the scenes the same way we'd been photographing the previous weeks, so after a while we forgot where we were and continued as if we were still working in Japan."

Marshall Herskovitz

武
士
道

109

Lilly Kilvert

Many weeks later, the team began filming in New Zealand, where preparation had been ongoing for over a year. "Geographically, New Zealand is very similar to Japan," notes Zwick. "They're both volcanic islands, at similar latitudes, on opposite sides of the equator— but New Zealand had the huge amount of open space that we needed, and the natural beauty to evoke a Japan that now exists only in myth."

Finding the locations was a pleasure for location manager Charlie Harrington. "Every morning for thirty days, I walked out of my hotel, got into the helicopter, and went sightseeing," Harrington says with a smile. "I scouted almost the entire country." Harrington was primarily searching for the location that would represent the visual heart of the story: Katsumoto's mountaintop village. He found the perfect site in the Taranaki region in the north. "I saw a place on a high plateau that looked like it could be on a mountainside, because it had elevated ground behind it. It just looked like the kind of terrain where samurai warriors would live. And the terrain made it possible to point the camera north, which was important for backlighting shots."

That northern sun was especially important to the director of photography, John Toll. "The direction of the natural light determined the direction we could shoot in," Toll says. "So the geography of the sets allowed us to maintain a certain lighting continuity. The New Zealand air is faultlessly clean and crisp," notes Toll, "so the sunlight is incredibly bright and 'contrasty.' That translates into

very hard shadows and very harsh daylight. We would be shooting during the summer months, when the days are very long and the sun is really high in the sky for a major part of the day. We looked for ways that we would be able to manipulate that light, by choosing film stock or by shooting in a particular direction. Of course," Toll adds, "because of the nature of New Zealand, sitting out there in the southern Pacific, it is very susceptible to changes in the weather. It can go from one extreme to the other in a matter of minutes, so maintaining lighting continuity was a real issue."

The rapid weather changes weren't only a lighting concern. After Zwick, Toll, and Kilvert approved the remote site for the village, they told the construction crew to "put in a road"— and that's when it started to rain. "At first we waited for the rain to stop," Harrington says. "But it didn't. It was the wettest winter in thirty years. Building the road turned into a night-mare of slush and mud."

The soggy production crew's first task was to plant the village gardens. "The gardens had to be period correct, so we planted vegetables, soybeans, rice, and tobacco," Kilvert says. In her determination to get it right, Kilvert "threatened people with bodily harm if they stepped off a path" while she made her gardens grow. "I yelled at everybody," she says with a grin. "But we shot there for six weeks without destroying the vegetation. We also planted over

a hundred trees, because there wasn't a tree in the entire valley when we got there. We put in pear trees and apple trees and cherry trees and pine trees and willow trees. And we transplanted a lot of bamboo."

The manufactured village eventually boasted thirty buildings of wood, bamboo, plaster, and stone scattered throughout the mile-long valley. "We manufactured the plaster from the mud right in the village," says art director Jess Gonchor. "A lot of the bamboo came from there, too. We even used rocks and wood that we collected in the valley, hoping that would help make the village look authentic. The elements of the weather aged all of the buildings by the time we started shooting, so it didn't look like a set. It looked as if it belonged there."

"About a week before we started shooting, Ed and Marshall and I just walked through the village by ourselves," recalls Tom Cruise. "We wandered around, looking at the details and discussing how they were made, and it was a wonderful afternoon, with the kind of feeling that makes you feel like a kid. We ate sandwiches and talked about the script, and then there was a moment when we all sat there quietly, just looking around. We knew what was ahead of us, and none of us was in a hurry to leave. It was a wonderful, wonderful moment."

The filmmaker's efforts were validated when actors from Japan arrived on the set for the first time. "They said it reminded them of the villages they had grown up in," says Kilvert, noting that she couldn't have asked for a better tribute than that.

111

ALLOW YOUR HEART
TO REMAIN AT EASE,
AND DESTINY WILL LEAD
THE WAY TO ACCORD
WITH OTHERS
THE WAY OF THE SAMURAI

EXT. ENCAMPMENT - NIGHT

> KATSUMOTO
> The emperor could not hear my words.
> His army will come. It is the end.

Algren just sits and listens.

> KATSUMOTO
> For 900 years my ancestors have protected
> our people. Now I have failed them.

> ALGREN
> So you will take your own life?

Katsumoto's silence is assent.

> ALGREN
> In shame?
>   (as Katsumoto says nothing)
> Shame for a life of service, discipline,
> compassion.

> KATSUMOTO
> The way of the samurai is not necessary
> anymore.

> ALGREN
>   (a rueful smile)
> Necessary? What could be more necessary?

> KATSUMOTO
> I will die by the sword. My own, or my
> enemies'.

> ALGREN
> Then let it be your enemies'. Together we
> will make the emperor hear you.

Katsumoto studies him, as if seeing him for the first
time.

Algren holds his look. The bond between them is now
complete.

INT. TAKA'S HOUSE - DUSK

Algren sits with the family in silence. Then:

> **HIGEN**
> (subtitles)
> Will you fight the white men, too?

> **ALGREN**
> (subtitles)
> If they come here, yes.

> **HIGEN**
> (subtitles)
> Why?

> **ALGREN**
> (subtitles)
> Because they come to destroy
> what I have come to love.

Taka looks at him, moved. Suddenly, Higen
jumps up and bolts out of the room. Algren
looks to Taka.

> **TAKA**
> (subtitles)
> The way of samurai is difficult
> for children. He misses his father.

> **ALGREN**
> (subtitles)
> And he is angry because I am the
> cause of that.

She smiles ever so slightly at his obliviousness.

> **TAKA**
> (subtitles)
> No. He is angry because he fears
> you will die as well.

116

COSTUMING THE PLAYERS—
THE KIMONO

The word *kimono* originally meant "clothing" in Japanese. But with the Westernization of Japanese culture, the word came to mean the "traditional" style of dress. This style first developed during the eighth and ninth centuries, as Japan was breaking free of the Chinese cultural influences it had followed up to that point. During that period, the "straight-line-cut method" of making clothing became popular. A piece of fabric 12 to 13 meters (39 to 43 feet) long and 36 to 40 centimeters (4 to 15 inches) wide was cut into eight smaller pieces, or panels, and then sewn back together in a basic form. There was no waste in this method, as every bit of fabric was used. Costume designer Ngila Dickson found it intriguing.

"The nature of the design is stunning," Dickson says. "Every kimono is constructed from the same-size piece of cloth, whether the kimono is for a child or an adult. It's like origami for clothing."

Over the centuries, styles and types of kimonos varied greatly, but for all that time, both men and women typically dressed in bright, even gaudy, colors. Then, during the eighth century, kimono makers developed new techniques for dyeing fabrics that for the first time allowed them to create a wide spectrum of subtle colors.

"During the Meiji period, the kimonos were incredibly subdued, both in pattern and in tone," Dickson says. "They came in rich, dark burgundy and indigo, and they were made from really beautiful silks and cottons. Ed Zwick and I just loved that look."

Working closely with wardrobe supervisor Akira Fukuda, the filmmakers searched throughout Japan, buying authentic period kimonos. "The merchants in Japan got to know us because we were the only tourists not going for bright, floral style or brocaded kimonos," Dickson says. "We were the ones looking for dark, beautifully textured kimonos and old boxes of original kimono rolls."

Still, they found it necessary to create the majority of the wardrobe themselves. "We were only interested in natural fabrics," Dickson says. "We worked with dyers and print-makers for months."

While researching the most important kimonos of all—those to be worn in the Imperial Court scenes—the filmmakers were introduced to Munehisa Sengoku, president of Japan's Institute of Court Culture. The gentleman, whose duties include managing the emperor's wardrobe, escorted them on a tour of the Imperial Museum, where he pointed out one very important fact—paintings of Japan's emperors cannot be taken at face value. "He explained to us that the artist would never have been allowed to actually see the emperor, so whatever clothing is in the painting is sometimes wrong," Dickson says. "And then he offered to make the emperor's costume for us for our very traditional scene."

The filmmakers were amazed by Sengoku's generosity—but it wasn't the only time the court official would surprise them. "I showed Sengoku Sensei a conceptual drawing of Katsumoto's most traditional garment, and he said, 'Let us make that for you, too,'" says Dickson. "Sometimes, when you're doing something special, the most extraordinary things happen."

武
士
道

119

武士道

武士道

COSTUMING THE PLAYERS: THE ARMOR

Unlike medieval European armor, which was forged out of solid metal, Japanese armor is composed of many individual "scales"—made from pieces of materials as diverse as copper and water buffalo hide—that are laced together with strips of deer hide. "It's very minimal," says costume designer Ngila Dickson. "Where it needs chain mail, it has chain mail. Where it doesn't need chain mail, there is something else. It's quite armadillo-like."

The complicated design requires the wearer to put on the various sections of armor in a very specific order. After putting on an intricate underlayer of garments that specifically correspond to the various parts of the armor itself, the warrior steps into his thigh-guards, or *haidate*, then puts on his gloves, the *yugake*. Next come the sleeves, or *kote*, the armpit protectors, or *wakibiki*, the breastplate, or *do* (which also includes shoulder plates), and finally the *uwa obi*, the belt that will hold his swords.

In making over three hundred suits of armor, says Dickson, "we found that there were no shortcuts. Because of the way the armor moves, even what goes underneath is as important as the armor that goes over it. And that made it feel authentic for the actors."

That authenticity was important to the filmmakers too, but for a different reason. "We were putting it on Japanese actors who have been portraying samurai for their entire careers," Dickson says, "so our hope was to get it just right. We were very open to the actors' comments and they worked very closely with us."

"The costume department gathered a great deal of research material," notes Ken Watanabe. "The colors and designs they chose were wonderful. But it would be us—the actors—who would have to wear the armor, so we requested modifications in such things as the shape of the armor, the texture of the glove, and the position and thickness of the lacing."

Watanabe also brought in even more research material—specifically on samurai helmets. "The armor and helmets not only signify strength, but are important for their aesthetic beauty. I wanted to relate this spirit by having Ngila look at a book about helmets and armor that was given to me by my teacher."

"Those helmets have a two-part purpose," Dickson notes. "They are meant to protect the head, obviously, but they're also meant to scare the living daylights out of the enemy."

Ngila Dickson

武士道

EXT. MOUNTAINS - DAY

Algren and Katsumoto look down into a valley.
Nakao and a few others wait at a discreet distance.

Below they see the Imperial Army, thousands
strong, marching across the valley toward them.
Terrifying martial columns in strict formation.
It is here that the final act of this inevitable drama
will play out…

              KATSUMOTO
You believe a man can change his destiny?

              ALGREN
I think a man does what he can, until his
destiny is revealed.

ALGREN (V.O.)
May 25, 1877. This will be the
last entry in this journal…

I have tried to give a true
accounting of what I have seen,
what I have done…

I do not presume to understand
the course of my life. I know I am
grateful to have partaken in
all this. Even if for a moment.

武士道

124

武
士
道
125

武士道

今古有神奉志士。

EXT. TAKA'S HOUSE - DAY

Katsumoto holds a beautiful samurai sword.

> KATSUMOTO
> You will need this.

He bows his head and offers it to Algren. There
are Japanese characters etched on the blade.

> ALGREN
> What does it say?

> KATSUMOTO
> "I belong to the warrior in whom
> the old ways have joined the new."

Katsumoto turns to the gathered samurai warriors
and calls out a battle cry. The samurai respond.

127

ARMING THE WARRIORS

"The sword is the soul of the samurai."
Torii Mototada
16th century

Weapons experts and historians agree that the Japanese sword is the ultimate cutting instrument. Early swordsmiths developed a complex method of combining steel and softer iron, so that the sword would have a hardened cutting edge encased in a resilient body. This allowed the samurai to block offensive blows with the back of the sword without fear of breaking the weapon. And when attacking, the sword's unique curved edge would first open a tiny slice that allowed the blade to continue through the flesh.

Swordsmiths hardened the blade using a layering process known as folding, in which the metal was forged to a high temperature, hammered until folded in half, and forged again until the surfaces fused together. Antique blades made during the late fourteenth and early fifteenth centuries by swordsmith Masamune Goro Nyudo are confirmed to have over four million folds, each serving as a microscopic cutting edge.

In *The Last Samurai,* translator Simon Graham tells Captain Algren that the samurai tested the sharpness of their swords by practicing on corpses. The filmmakers didn't have that option, so they chose the second-best method—slicing through rolled up tatami, Japanese straw floor mats. The practicing swordsman would roll the mat tightly until it was the diameter of a human neck. Then he would stand it upright and slice through it.

武
士
道

"We had a sword master who did this on film for us," producer Marshall Herskovitz says. "In one take, the sliver of mat he cut was very thin, and it didn't even wobble. It sat there as if he had missed the mat entirely. Then he just reached out and flipped it away with his finger. It was really quite remarkable."

Not all of the swords used in the movie were that authentic. "We also had plastic swords and aluminum swords, rubber swords and bamboo swords," Herskovitz notes.

"We used a total of seven hundred swords," says property master Dave Gulick, the man in charge of the film's bladed weapons. "Each samurai needed a *katana*, or long sword, a *wakizachi*, or short sword, and a dagger called a *tanto*."

Gulick and his staff cast replicas of antique weapons, some of which were three hundred years old. Swords weren't the only weapons required for the project. The property department manufactured two hundred bows from bamboo, laminating and lacquering the wood exactly as had been done by the samurai for hundreds of years. Archery had been the samurai's highest discipline during the

seventh and eighth centuries. These warriors, known as *ashigaru*, referred to their specialty as "The Way of the Bow and the Horse," because they developed firing techniques while practicing on horseback.

"We found authentic bows from the period and reproduced them. And once we had the bows, we needed arrows—so we made seven thousand of them!" Gulick says. "The actors fired many of the arrows, but we also used a lot of them for set dressing on the battlefields, where we had a hundred and forty dead bodies and twenty dead horses"—all manufactured by the prop crew, of course.

"We made spears too, which are called *nagae-yari*," Gulick continues. "And leather quivers for the archers to wear. And we made scabbards for all the swords out of hard polyurethane.

"But of all the weapons-related props, Algren's sword was my favorite," Gulick concludes. "We consulted with a scholar in Japan to find the best way to inscribe the words— 'I belong to the warrior in whom the old ways have joined the new'—on it. That sword is one of the best things in the film."

武士道

SAMURAI BATTLE SKILLS

The samurai customarily wore two swords. In times of war, it was his duty to do so. Each sword served its own purpose. The warrior might choose his *wakizachi*, or short sword, when fighting in confined spaces. But on the battlefield, he drew his *katana*, or long sword— his ultimate killing instrument.

Swordsmanship, or *kenjutsu* (which developed into modern *kendo*), was not the samurai class's original fighting method of choice. Over the years, techniques of war evolved—from the Way of the Bow, to the Way of the Spear, to the Way of the Sword. Archery, or *kyujutsu*, was Japan's first martial art, and as a combat technique typically was combined with *bajutsu*, or horsemanship. Following the introduction of the gun

to Japan in the sixteenth century, however, cavalrymen found that sitting high in the saddle while firing arrows made them easy targets for trained riflemen. Because of this, riders all but abandoned the bow in favor of the *mochi-yari*— the "held spear."

The spear was an all-purpose weapon that could be used on horseback or on foot. In one well-known horseback technique, the mounted samurai would charge in such a way as to keep his opponent on his left. While grasping the reins in his left hand, he would hold the spear horizontally across his body with his right, and jab the opponent as they passed. A different spear technique worked when a samurai found himself surrounded by conscripted foot soldiers, whose traditional weapons were long, pointed pikes. He would hold the spear near the end of the shaft and whirl it around in a wide circle, the head of the spear deflecting the pikes as he raced through them.

Young samurai used many techniques to learn swordsmanship. To improve their footwork and timing, they would hang small objects at various levels from tree branches with string, set the suspended objects in motion, and then attempt to touch them all without losing balance or control. They used bamboo or wooden swords for this exercise, so as not to slice the string. In the winter, they would strengthen their legs by lurching through deep snowdrifts while swinging their heavy *katanas*.

The *katana* was a two-handed weapon, although especially skilled warriors occasionally wielded it with one hand or even fought with a sword in each hand. With its curved blade, it was a "slashing" weapon rather than a "stabbing" weapon. There were only five classic positions, or stances, from which to strike. In the "upper"

From each of these five stances, an infinite number of variations could be devised. The swordsman's trick was to keep his opponent, standing a mere sword-length away, unaware of his position. Each fighter attempted to take "the stance of no stance," by moving casually and remaining calm. An expert swordsman might even leave his sword in its scabbard, with the intention of drawing it at the last moment. This "quick draw" technique was known as *iaijutsu*, and it entailed drawing the sword, killing the opponent with a single blow and returning the sword smoothly to the scabbard.

As each opponent attempted to prevent the other from surmising whether he was in a defensive or offensive position, deception became as important as the blade. In one famous recorded incident, Yagyu Jubei, the master swordsman of the Tokugawa government, was accosted by a large band of cutthroats while walking in a dark area of Kyoto. The outlaws demanded that he give them his overcoat and his swords. Jubei removed his coat, but when one of the robbers

position, the samurai held his sword overhead, with the blade pointed toward the opponent's eyes, at the ready to deflect the opponent's blade. In the "middle" position, he again held his blade overhead, with the intention of striking the opponent's body rather than his blade. In the "lower" position, he held his sword low, below the opponent's sword, prepared to strike the opponent's hands and arms. In the "left" position, the samurai held his sword horizontally to the left side, thus allowing him to deflect the attacking sword from below before slicing diagonally upward across the opponent's body. And in the "right" position, he held his sword horizontally on his right side, with the intention of swinging it into the "upper" position before slicing downward across the opponent.

reached out to take it, Jubei dropped it. The man's eyes followed the coat as it fell, whereupon the samurai drew his sword and cut down the robber. Many others rushed forward to avenge their dead accomplice. Jubei struck down twelve of them before the others fled in panic. Deception, the "quick draw," and expert swordsmanship had saved his life—and his overcoat.

On the battlefield, the concept of keeping one's distance—but not *too* much distance—was especially critical. Ideally, the samurai would stand at exactly the length of his opponent's sword, plus a little more—less than one inch. This "margin of safety" made all the difference in a fight, for if a swordsman took the initiative and swung his *katana*, only to miss, his opponent easily found the time to move in for the kill.

131

EXT. CANNON HILL - CONTINUOUS

A moment of stillness on both ends of the field.
Bagley, Omura and several German and Japanese
officers stand atop the ridge among the cannon.

武士道

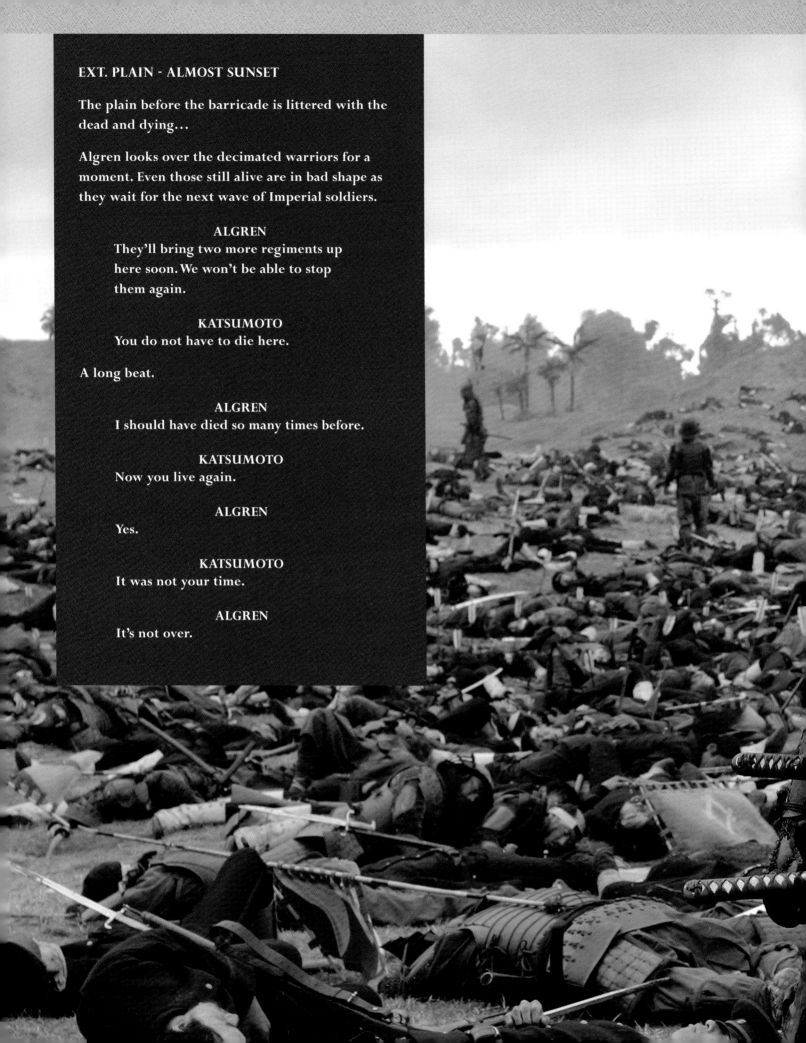

EXT. PLAIN - ALMOST SUNSET

The plain before the barricade is littered with the dead and dying…

Algren looks over the decimated warriors for a moment. Even those still alive are in bad shape as they wait for the next wave of Imperial soldiers.

> ALGREN
> They'll bring two more regiments up here soon. We won't be able to stop them again.

> KATSUMOTO
> You do not have to die here.

A long beat.

> ALGREN
> I should have died so many times before.

> KATSUMOTO
> Now you live again.

> ALGREN
> Yes.

> KATSUMOTO
> It was not your time.

> ALGREN
> It's not over.

EXT. PLAIN – SUNSET

The hundred mounted samurai move through the smoke and flames like horsemen of the apocalypse.

Katsumoto and Algren lead them.

EXT. PLAIN - SUNSET

Katsumoto points his sword
and screams out his war cry.

The samurai horsemen
begin to walk forward...

And then to canter...

CANNONS FIRE.

And they charge.

It is suicidal.

It is glorious.

It is the end of the samurai.

Algren draws his sword.

150
武士道

TRAINING THE HORSES

Horse wrangler Pete White received his assignment a year before the start of principal photography: Assemble a herd of sixty horses and train them to perform difficult stunts under "battle conditions"—gunfire, explosions, hand-to-hand combat—not to mention the general chaos of filmmaking going on around them. In spite of White's previous work on such films as *Pride and Prejudice* and even *Gladiator*—where the horses had to encounter tigers and fire—this task represented a real challenge.

"Nothing I'd done before was this intensive," says White. "We had never asked this much from our animals."

"We looked at over two thousand horses around New Zealand's north island in order to find the sixty head we needed," White recalls. "None of the horses had ever been on a film set before. They were all doing different jobs, like herding stock or working on farms or orchards, and a couple of them had been racehorses, had played polo or had worked in riding schools."

Before long, dozens of horse trailers converged on the farm where White set up his training center. "A lot of the horses were a bit stale and

weren't physically fit when we started," White says. "But we took them through a three-month training period, and by the time we finished shooting the movie, they were almost good enough to go on the track."

White and his eighteen-person crew of wranglers and stunt trainers set up an obstacle course dubbed "the desensitization lane," and draped it with flapping flags and streamers, scattered filmmaking equipment and a smoke-making machine. "We rode the horses through there three times a day to get them used to it," White says.

"And we played polo with them, using sticks and a huge beach ball. The horses got used to being maneuvered one-handed, and pushing into one another with that big ball bouncing around them. It was the closest thing to a battle atmosphere without being too intense. And since it was more like playing a sport than doing a job, the horses really came to enjoy it."

After that, White adds, "We started setting off explosions and gunfire a good distance away, and bringing the sounds closer every day. Then we began to carry starter pistols, so they heard the sound of gunfire from within their work area as well. Eventually they became so at ease with the noise that you could start firing right next to them and the horses wouldn't even look."

The crew selected specific horses to perform stunts, such as jumping, rearing, and falling. And it was the "falling horses" that proved to be White's favorite stunt. "It was very impressive," the trainer says. "We started by showing the horses how to bend down on one shoulder, and then to roll. We taught them very slowly. As they got used to it, we advanced to having them go down at a walk, then a trot, a canter and finally at a gallop.

"We taught them to lie on the floor for five minutes each time they did the stunt, so that they wouldn't instantly jump up among pieces of the set or among the crew members, and get hurt or hurt somebody. Keeping them down that long was the hardest part. Horses are 'flight animals,' so lying down is not a natural thing. It took about six weeks to build up their confidence to the point that they knew they were safe down there. But we got them to relax and just lie there while other horses and guys with swords were running around them. After each of the stunt horses had done it about two hundred

times, it actually became a job for us to get them back off the floor after two or three minutes had gone by," White says with a chuckle. "They became so relaxed that they probably thought, 'Yeah, this is quite nice down here.'"

Producer Herskovitz took a special interest in the horse training. "I fell in love with riding while we were doing *Legends of the Fall,* and I've ridden seriously ever since. Pete's dedication, his patience, and his love for those horses was nothing short of astonishing." Every possible precaution was taken to protect the equine performers, including the use of dummy horses for the most dangerous stunts, and an animatronic, computer-controlled horse for Tom Cruise's most dangerous stunt—the "T-bone" sequence—when his horse is broadsided by another horse. White is particularly proud of his team's effort in creating the final horse-charge sequence in the film. And nothing pleases him more than the fact that after thirty days of filming—under the constant vigilance of the New Zealand Film and Television Unit of the American Humane Association—and after literally hundreds of explosions and squibs and falls, not one horse suffered an injury.

153

武
士
道

EXT. BATTLEFIELD - CHERRY TREES - SUNSET

Katsumoto reaches out, struggling for Algren's short sword. Algren places his hand on Katsumoto's arm preventing him from taking the sword.

> **KATSUMOTO**
> You have your honor again. Let me die with mine…

Algren looks at him, deeply moved.

> **KATSUMOTO**
> Help me up.

Algren helps him, supporting Katsumoto as he holds the sword's point to his stomach.

Algren tightly grasps the sword.

> **ALGREN**
> Are you ready?

In Katsumoto's eyes, a resolute and calm acceptance of death.

Algren looks at him deeply, warmly.

> **ALGREN**
> I will miss our conversations.

Katsumoto embraces Algren firmly -- the small sword impales him -- Algren holds him tightly. Katsumoto is looking over Algren's shoulder as he is dying. Cherry blossoms. A display of perfect beauty. A look of joy and absolute peace comes to his features.

> **KATSUMOTO**
> (whispers)
> Perfect… They are all perfect.

His eyes close. He is dead. Algren gently kneels with Katsumoto's body.

The Japanese officer just looks over the plain of dying samurai for a moment. Then he does the most remarkable thing.

He slowly kneels and touches his head to the dirt.

Then a soldier near him does the same thing. Then another and another. And then by the thousands.

They kneel and touch their heads to the dirt.

Honoring the last samurai.

武士道

155

INT. IMPERIAL PALACE - THRONE ROOM - DAY

Algren enters with Graham. He is limping and a bloodstain is beginning to seep through his shirt. He carries something wrapped in a blanket.

It is Katsumoto's long samurai sword.

He prostrates himself at the emperor's feet. Algren unwraps the bundle and remains prostrate with his head bowed as he offers up the sword.

> OMURA
> (subtitles)
> Highness, if we could just conclude the matter at hand…

> ALGREN
> (ignoring Omura)
> This is Katsumoto's sword. He would have wanted you to have it -- that the strength of the samurai be with you always…

> OMURA
> (subtitles)
> Enlightened One, we all weep for Katsumoto, but…

> ALGREN
> He hoped, with his last breath, that you would remember all the ancestors who held this sword, and what they died for.

> EMPEROR
> (to Algren)
> You were with him at the end.

> ALGREN
> *Hai.*

> OMURA
> Emperor, this man fought against you.

> ALGREN
> Your Highness, if you believe me to be your enemy -- command me -- and I will gladly take my life.

The emperor is stunned to hear this from a Westerner. Then he makes a decision that will change his life. He stands.

> EMPEROR
> I have dreamed of a unified Japan. Of a country strong and independent and modern… And now we have railroads and cannon and Western clothing.
> (touches the sword lovingly)
> But we cannot forget who we are. Or where we come from.

INT. LECTURE HALL (ENGLAND) - DAY

GRAHAM

And in the years to come Japan would chart a stormy course into the modern age. Nations, like men, it is sometimes said, have their own destiny...

As for the American captain, no one knows what became of him. All that remains is his journal -- which I have published, according to his last request.
(beat)
Some say that he died of his wounds, others that he returned to his own country...

But I like to think he may have found at last some small measure of the peace that we all seek, and few of us ever find.

Time Inc. HOME ENTERTAINMENT

President Rob Gursha
Vice President, Branded Businesses David Arfine
Vice President, New Product Development Richard Fraiman
Executive Director, Marketing Services Carol Pittard
Director, Retail & Special Sales Tom Mifsud
Director of Finance Tricia Griffin
Prepress Manager Emily Rabin
Book Production Manager Jonathan Polsky
Associate Product Manager Victoria Alfonso

special thanks
Bozena Bannett, Alex Bliss, Robert Dente, Gina Di Meglio,
Anne-Michelle Gallero, Peter Harper, Suzanne Janso,
Robert Marasco, Natalie McCrea, Mary Jane Rigoroso,
Steven Sandonato, Grace Sullivan

Published by Time Inc. Home Entertainment

Time Inc.
1271 Avenue of the Americas
New York, New York 10020

For Roundtable Press, Inc.
Directors Julie Merberg and Marsha Melnick
Executive Editor Patty Brown
Editor John Glenn
Associate Editor Sara Newberry
Design Jon Glick, Mouse + Tiger Design
Research and sidebar text Terry J. Erdmann

ISBN: 1-932273-30-1
Library of Congress Control Number: 2003105222

Time Inc. Home Entertainment is a subsidiary of Time Inc.

If you would like to order *The Last Samurai*, please call us
at 1-800-327-6388 (Monday through Friday, 7:00 A.M.—
8:00 P.M. or Saturday, 7:00 A.M.— 6:00 P.M. Central Time).

武士道